Made in the USA
Monee, IL
19 May 2022

96730726R00233